STEM Projects in **MINECRAFT**™

The Unofficial Guide to
Raising Animals in
MINECRAFT™

JILL KEPPELER AND SAM KEPPELER

PowerKiDS press.

New York

Published in 2019 by The Rosen Publishing Group, Inc.
29 East 21st Street, New York, NY 10010

First Edition

Editor: Greg Roza
Book Design: Rachel Rising
Illustrator: Matías Lapegüe

Photo Credits: Cover, pp. 1, 3, 4, 6, 8, 10, 12, 14, 16, 18, 20, 22, 23, 24 (background) Evgeniy Dzyuba/Shutterstock.com; pp. 4, 6, 8, 12, 14, 16, 18 (insert) Levent Konuk/Shutterstock.com; p. 5 symbiot/Shutterstock.com; p. 7 nekomamire/Shutterstock.com; p. 9 Berna Namoglu/Shutterstock.com; p. 11 The Len/Shutterstock.com; p. 13 Olga_i/Shutterstock.com; p. 15 olgaru79/Shutterstock.com; p. 17 Josh Cornish/Shutterstock.com; p. 21 Alexey Seafarer/Shutterstock.com; p. 22 Hogan Imaging/Shutterstock.com.

Library of Congress Cataloging-in-Publication Data

Names: Keppeler, Jill, author.
Title: The unofficial guide to raising animals in Minecraft / Jill Keppeler
   and Sam Keppeler.
Description: New York : PowerKids Press, [2019] | Series: STEM projects in
   Minecraft | Includes index.
Identifiers: LCCN 2018028495| ISBN 9781538342541 (library bound) | ISBN
   9781538342527 (paperback) | ISBN 9781538342534 (6 pack)
Subjects: LCSH: Animal culture–Juvenile literature. |
   Livestock–Growth–Juvenile literature. | Minecraft (Game)–Juvenile
   literature.
Classification: LCC SF75.5 .K46 2019 | DDC 636–dc23
LC record available at https://lccn.loc.gov/2018028495

Manufactured in the United States of America

CPSIA Compliance Information: Batch #CWPK19. For Further Information contact Rosen Publishing, New York, New York at 1-800-237-9932

Contents

Cows and Llamas and Wolves, Oh My!

We share our world with many creatures, both wild and tame. The world of *Minecraft* is no different! There aren't nearly as many animals, but just like in the real world, they all have different **traits** and native **biomes**. There are animals that can help you survive and animals you'll want to avoid.

Minecraft has animals such as cows and chickens that can provide you with food. It has animals such as donkeys and llamas that can carry your stuff. It even has pets such as cats and parrots. Read on to find out more about the wild world of *Minecraft* animals!

MINECRAFT MANIA

In *Minecraft,* a moving creature that isn't a player is called a mob. Animals are mobs. So are *Minecraft's* monsters!

Just like in real life, *Minecraft* cows are a source of milk and food!

Tame or Wild?

Some of the animals we have in our real world can be tamed so that they live and work with humans. Some animals will always be wild. It's the same in *Minecraft*. Some mobs can be tamed and some can't.

Of the animals that can't be tamed, some mobs are passive. This means they never hurt a *Minecraft* player. Some are neutral. This means they won't hurt a player unless the player does something to them or there are other certain **circumstances**. Some are hostile. Most hostile mobs are monsters, but some tamable or neutral mobs can become hostile.

MINECRAFT MANIA

Spiders and cave spiders are *Minecraft* monsters, but they're only hostile during the night or if a player attacks them. They're much bigger than real-word spiders!

Minecraft squids can look scary, but they're passive mobs. They'll never hurt you. They only spawn, or appear, in water, and if you kill them, they drop ink sacs.

Useful Livestock

Minecraft's livestock animals include cows, sheep, pigs, and chickens. You can find these animals in almost any biome. They can all provide a player with meat, and all except pigs provide other **resources** as well. When killed, cows drop meat and leather. You can also milk them if you have a bucket. Pigs provide pork chops. Chickens drop feathers (used to make arrows) and raw chicken meat.

Sheep drop mutton, or sheep meat, and wool if you kill them. But it's better to make shears, or clippers, with two iron **ingots** and use those instead. Then you can shear a sheep for its wool again and again!

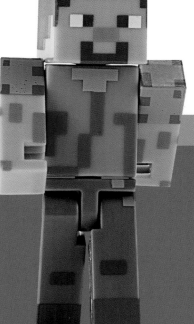

MINECRAFT MANIA

Drinking milk in *Minecraft* will cure poisoning from cave spiders, witches, or other sources. You can use wool to make beds, carpets, and banners. Leather is used for armor!

If you cut off a *Minecraft* sheep's wool, it will soon eat a patch of grass and regrow its wool. In the real world, people shear sheep too. This lets us use the wool and keeps the sheep cooler in warm weather.

SHEEP

SHEARED SHEEP

Down on the Farm

If you want to keep *Minecraft* livestock handy so you have a steady supply of resources, you can make your own farm. With wood planks and sticks, you can create fences and gates to make a pen to hold the animals. Unlike real animals, *Minecraft* animals don't need to be kept warm or dry, so you don't have to make a roof or walls. You can if you want, though!

You can draw animals to your pen with seeds of any sort (for chickens), wheat (for cows or sheep), or potatoes, carrots, or beetroots (for pigs). These animals will follow players who are holding those items.

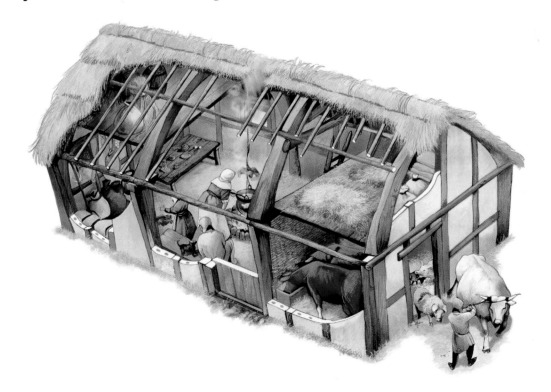

Minecraft chickens lay eggs every five to 10 minutes. If you have a pen full of chickens, you can collect lots of eggs! They can be used in some *Minecraft* recipes, such as the one below.

PUMPKIN

SUGAR

EGG

PUMPKIN PIE

Baby Critters

For many kinds of *Minecraft* animals (except spiders, cave spiders, bats, parrots, and squids), there are baby **versions**. You can breed the adult versions of most of these animals, which means you can cause them to make a baby animal. The babies grow into adult animals.

To do this, feed two adult animals their favorite type of food. These are the same foods you can draw them in with. For tamed wolves, use any kind of meat. For cats, use raw fish. Tamed llamas can be bred using hay bales, and tamed horses and donkeys need golden apples or golden carrots. To breed rabbits, use carrots or flowers.

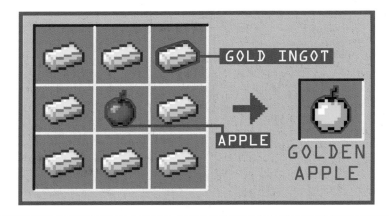

MINECRAFT MANIA

To make a golden apple, you need an apple and eight gold ingots. To make a golden carrot, you need a carrot and eight golden nuggets, or small pieces of gold.

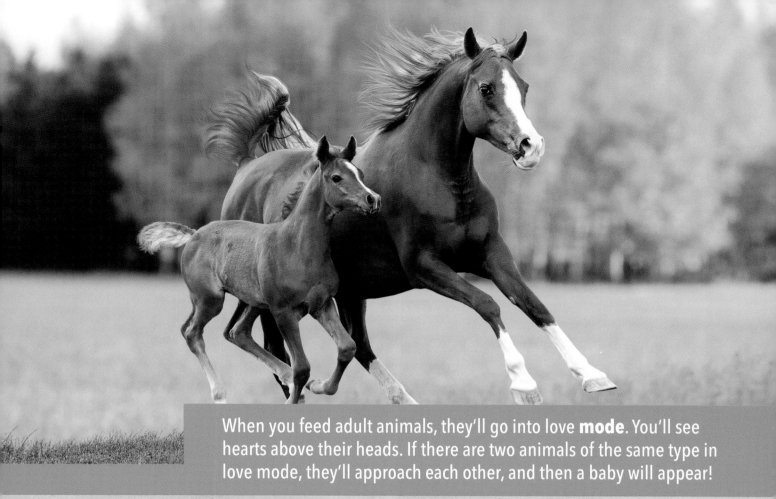

When you feed adult animals, they'll go into love **mode**. You'll see hearts above their heads. If there are two animals of the same type in love mode, they'll approach each other, and then a baby will appear!

Ride Like the Wind

One of the most useful mobs in *Minecraft* is the horse. You can tame horses and ride them if you have a saddle. It's much faster than walking. However, you can only find horses in plains and **savanna** biomes. They're almost always in herds, just like real horses!

To tame a horse (or a donkey), you must make sure your hands are empty. Click on the horse to get onto its back. It might throw you off! If it does, keep trying until you see hearts over the horse's head. Now, it's tamed. You can put a saddle on it to ride it or leash it with a lead.

MINECRAFT MANIA

You can even put armor on your horse! However, you can only find saddles or horse armor in chests in special *Minecraft* locations such as villages, jungle or desert temples, or **dungeons**.

Minecraft horses, like real horses, come in many patterns and colors. There are 35 possible color and pattern combinations in the game. This horse is an Appaloosa. Appaloosa horses have small spots.

Pack Animals

Some *Minecraft* animals can carry your stuff! This is useful when you're moving many resources. Donkeys often spawn when horses do. They can carry chests that hold 15 items or stacks of items. They're a little smaller than horses and you can tame them the same way.

Llamas are another *Minecraft* pack animal. You can only find them in savanna **plateaus** and **extreme** hills biomes. You can tame llamas just like horses and leash and lead them. If you lead one tamed llama, all the other llamas in the area will follow it! If all the llamas are carrying chests, you can move a lot of stuff this way.

MINECRAFT MANIA

Llamas in *Minecraft* spit, just like real llamas! They'll spit if a player or another mob attacks them.

Minecraft Llamas come in four colors: white, off-white, brown, and gray. In the real world, llamas often live in the high places of South America. People often use them as pack animals.

Man's Best Friends

You can have pets in *Minecraft*, too! You can find wolves in forest and **taiga** biomes. Tame them by feeding them bones (which you get by killing skeletons) until you see hearts. Tamed wolves have collars and will attack mobs that attack their owner. Wild wolves, however, will attack you if you hurt one of them.

Ocelots are a type of wild cat you can only find in *Minecraft* jungles. These yellow, spotted cats are rare and shy! If you can get close enough, you can feed them raw fish until you tame them. Then they have one of three different coat patterns. Creepers avoid cats!

MINECRAFT MANIA

Parrots are a flying *Minecraft* mob that you can only find in jungles. They come in five different colors and you can tame them by feeding them seeds.

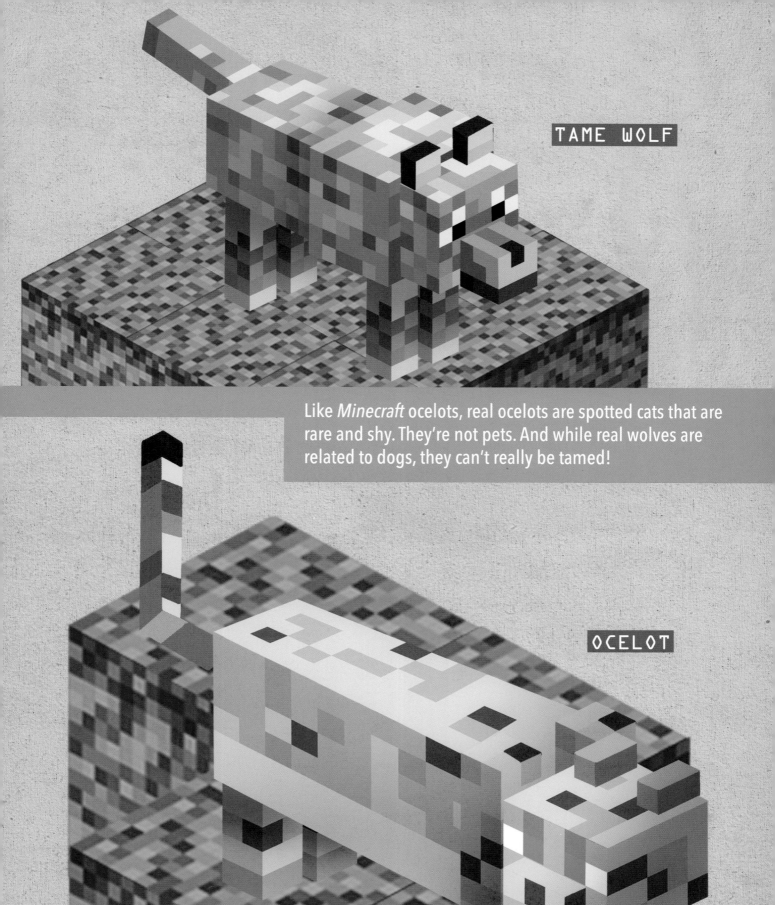

TAME WOLF

Like *Minecraft* ocelots, real ocelots are spotted cats that are rare and shy. They're not pets. And while real wolves are related to dogs, they can't really be tamed!

OCELOT

19

The Wild Ones

There are a few other animal mobs in *Minecraft*, but they can't be tamed and they're not livestock. Bats are a flying, passive mob. They spawn in caves. Rabbits are small, passive mobs that spawn in multiple biomes. They're cute and speedy and come in many colors, but if you can bring yourself to kill one, they drop rabbit skin and rabbit meat.

Polar bears only spawn in biomes with lots of snow and ice. The cubs are passive and the adults are neutral, but if you attack an adult—or get too close to a polar bear cub—they'll become hostile!

In *Minecraft*, polar bears, when hostile, are very dangerous to players because they're powerful and can swim faster than players. In real life, polar bears can grow up to 1,600 pounds (725.7 kg) and are very good swimmers!

Making Mods

You can make your *Minecraft* creations even more exciting with modifications, or mods. Using a computer program called ScriptCraft, you can create new blocks, change the way the game functions, and make your own games. Imagine what you could create! Would you like to make new *Minecraft* animals, such as elephants or foxes? What about changing existing mobs to make tamable monsters?

If you're interested in learning how to create mods in *Minecraft*, visit the website below. You'll find the information needed to get started with ScriptCraft and build your own *Minecraft* mods.

https://scriptcraftjs.org/

Glossary

biome: A natural community of plants and animals, such as a forest or desert.

circumstance: A condition, fact, or event.

dungeon: A dark, underground prison.

extreme: Existing to a very high degree.

ingot: Metal made into a shape for storage or transportation.

mode: A form of something that is different from other forms of the same thing.

plateau: A large area of land with raised sides and a level top.

resource: Something that can be used.

savanna: A grassland with scattered patches of trees.

taiga: A forest near the Arctic region that has many evergreen trees.

trait: A quality that makes one person or thing different from another.

version: A form of something that is different from the ones that came before it.

Index

Websites